Born A Barista A true story

Dedication

I dedicate this to my daughter, Kiana. I am proud of who you are growing up to be and pray God will guide your every path.

Acknowledgment

Meet Kiana, the cutest little five-year-old with a heart full of cozy vibes! She's a fan of all things sweet and snuggly: coffee, hot cocoa, and a mountain of cookies, cakes and cupcakes!

MENU

Kianas
cupcakes

Kiana's mom did not understand why her daughter liked coffee so much if she never tasted it.

 "It smells so good, Mommy!" yelled Kiana. "And people get together and hang out, and I like that," Kiana said.

At the supermarket Kiana's mom always bought coffee cups, coffee, cocoa, chocolate, and cake mix so she could create different things for her pretend cafe.

Coffee

When they got home Kiana's mother taught her how to make her own menu for her pretend cafe on the computer.

They looked at different cakes, cupcakes and designs for a menu. Kiana was happy.

MENU

Kiana's mother saw she wanted to be a barista and have her own coffee shop, but she wanted her to be a teacher like her.

"Nena you should be a teacher!"

Kiana did not want to be a teacher like her mother.

"But I want to make coffee,
cakes, cupcakes, and cocoa,"
Kiana would say to her mother.

Kiana got older. Every day for years, Kiana was on the computer learning about cake, cupcake, and cookie recipes. She learned about different coffees too.
She was happy.

Coffee

Kiana dreamed of having her own café and thought about different names for her café, like Kiana's Creations or Kiana's Anime Coffee Shop.

KIANA'S COOL
CAFE

"Kiana, you should sing and play guitar," her father said.

"But I want to make coffee, cakes, cupcakes and cocoa," said Kiana.

Kiana's younger brother Elias said, "You should be a personal trainer and you would be super healthy like me!"

"But I want to make coffee, cakes, cupcakes and cocoa," said Kiana.

Kiana worked at a grocery store, a Dominican restaurant, and she wanted nothing more than to work at a coffee shop.

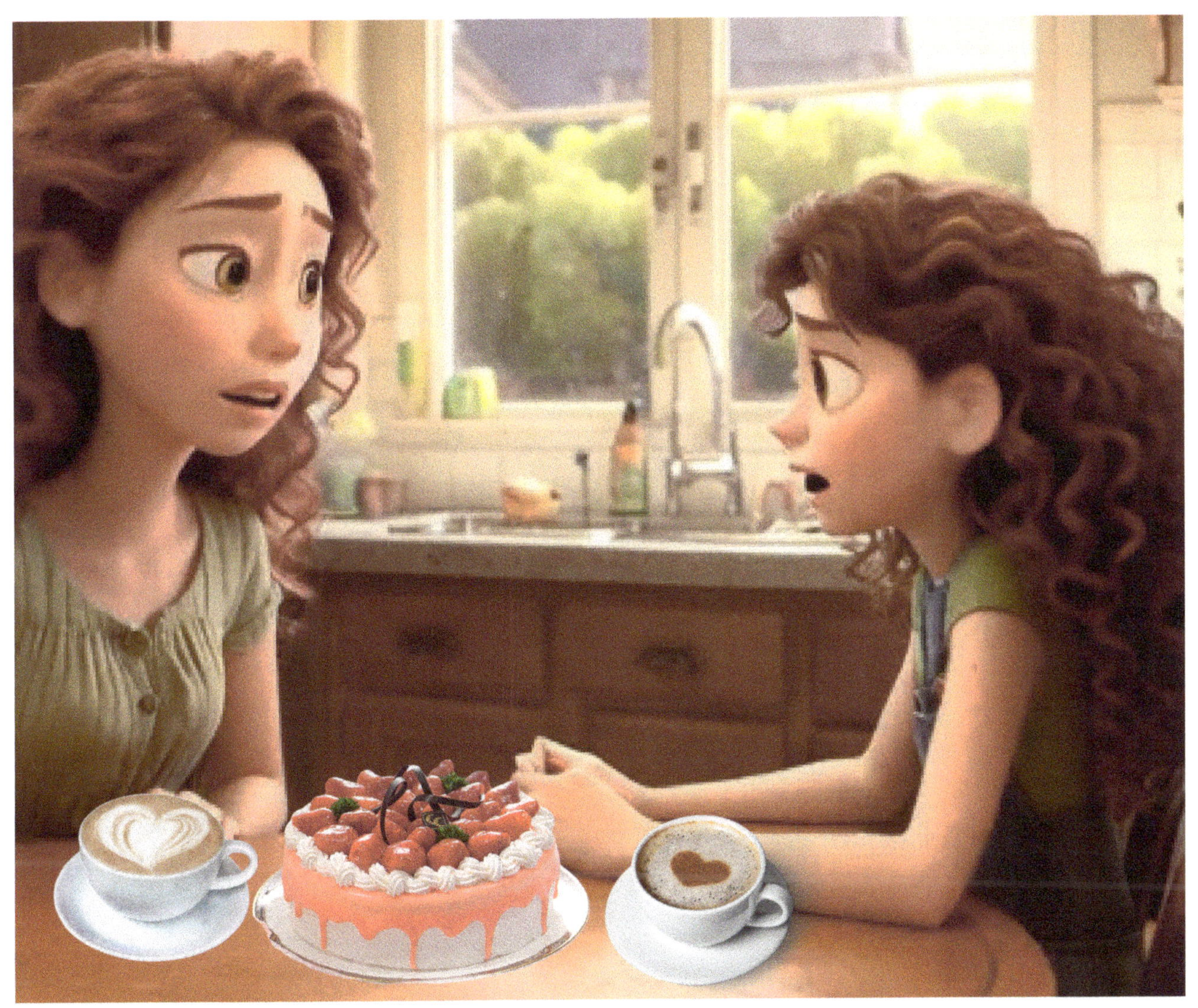

When she got older she asked her mother to get her
a job at a coffee shop so she can get paid for doing
something she loves.

Kiana's mother told her to check her phone because someone would call her soon.

THE
next
DAY

Kiana was hired at a famous French coffee shop and she was serving cakes and making coffees and teas, and was so happy! She did not have to be a teacher, a guitarist, or a personal trainer.

hello
MY NAME IS
Kiana

Questions

1. **What was the main character's name?**
2. **What did she want to do when she was little?**
3. **What did her mom want her to do?**
4. **What did Kiana respond?**
5. **What did her dad want her to do?**
6. **What was her response to her dad?**
7. **What did her brother think she should do? Why?**
8. **What do you want to do?**